TREASURED LANDSCAPES

TREASURED LANDSCAPES:

NATIONAL PARK SERVICE
Art Collections Tell America's Stories

TREASURED LANDSCAPES:
National Park Service
Art Collections Tell America's Stories

Published by the National Park Service
Museum Management Program
In celebration of the
National Park Service Centennial 1916–2016
with the companion virtual exhibition at
www.nps.gov/museum

Joan Bacharach, General Editor, Exhibit Curator and
Project Manager, and written together with museum
staff at over 45 National Parks
Amber Dumler, Designer

Published by the National Park Service
Museum Management Program
Washington, D.C.
2016

ISBN: 978-0-692-53608-7
Library of Congress Control Number: 2015953396

Front cover: **(Grand Canyon Scene at Eastern End of Canyon)** Thomas Moran, 1920 | Oil on canvas. W 101.7, H 77 cm | Grand Canyon National Park, GRCA 13630

Frontispiece: **The Yellowstone Range from Near Fort Ellis,** Thomas Moran, 1871 | Watercolor, gouache and pencil on paper. H 25, W 34.5 cm | Yellowstone National Park, YELL 8531

Formal titles for the artworks are in bold. Works without a formal title are in bold with the subject description in parentheses. 2016 v2.

Contents

Green River Cliffs Thomas Moran, 1920 | Oil on canvas. H 48.4, W 62.7 cm | National Park Service, Museum Management Program, WASO 1447

Overview

"Perception of beauty, and action to preserve and create it, are a fundamental test of a great society."   Laurance S. Rockefeller, White House Conference on Natural Beauty, 1965

Paintings, watercolors, sketches, and other works on paper from over 45 National Park Service collections are seen together here for the first time to illustrate and tell the story of the Service's first 100 years. Assembled to commemorate the National Park Service Centennial, 1916–2016, the magnificent works of art in this book and companion virtual exhibit celebrate the remarkable diversity of the national parks and National Park Service museum collections, as well as the richness of artists' encounters with the landscape.

Each park has its own mission, but all share the goal of preserving the nation's natural and cultural heritage. The artwork in each park's museum collection reflects that park's unique history and mission. These works capture awe-inspiring landscapes, honor individuals who have contributed to the nation's identity, and commemorate inspiring American ideas and events.

Landscape art played a major role in the establishment of the National Park Service. The works of art that are featured here follow in that great tradition. All fall within a broad definition of landscape art. Each work of art is connected to the land and nature in one form or another. The works include traditional landscapes that capture monumental views and natural phenomena; solitary figures dwarfed by nature; people outdoors, including armies—both on the move and in camp; waterscapes framed by land, some featuring

individuals at the water's edge; homes and towns set within the cultural landscape; distant horizons viewed from confinement; rustic sylvan scenes; and wildlife within their habitats. Together, they convey a captivating record of the nation's heritage and reveal the fascinating history of the National Park Service.

Three themes are highlighted in this book and the companion virtual exhibit. The first theme depicts America's treasured landscapes. Artists, in particular landscape painters such as Thomas Moran and others, inspired national leaders to protect and preserve these special places for all Americans. Their efforts led to the establishment of Yellowstone, the country's first national park. The second theme highlights landscape art displayed in the homes of eminent Americans. These works reflect the personal taste and private lives of public figures who have contributed to and shaped the nation's history. The third theme focuses on the artworks that mirror the broad range of American experiences. From war and confinement, to experiencing nature, these artworks document experiences that have molded America's character.

The works of art in National Park Service museum collections invite exploration of grand American places and connection with iconic Americans and experiences through the nation's "greatest idea," the National Park System.

Landscape Art and the Founding of the National Park Service

"... to conserve the scenery and the natural and historic objects and the wild life therein and to provide for the enjoyment of the same in such manner and by such means as will leave them unimpaired for the enjoyment of future generations." National Park Service Organic Act, 1916

Art—in particular, landscape art and photography—were crucial to the establishment of the National Park Service. Artist George Caitlin first conceived of the national park idea in 1832. He envisioned large-scale natural preservation for public enjoyment as he traveled to the American interior to paint portraits of Native Americans. Concerned about the destructive effects of westward expansion, Caitlin wanted "by some great protecting policy of government … a magnificent park … a nation's park, containing man and beast, in all the wild (ness) and freshness of their nature's beauty!"

Landscape paintings and photographs captured the grandeur and beauty of the West and captivated audiences at a time when travel was limited. These artworks created a groundswell of support to preserve natural wonders that culminated in the establishment of the National Park Service in 1916.

Romantic portrayals of nature by artists, including Thomas Cole and Frederick Edwin Church, countered earlier views of the wilderness as something to be conquered. As appreciation for what was perceived as unspoiled nature grew and as spectacular Western natural areas became known, the idea of preserving such places began to take hold. The American public first saw Yosemite Falls when a drawing, *The High Fall* by Thomas Ayres, was published in 1856. This, together with Carleton Watkins' mammoth photographs of Yosemite in 1861, stimulated interest in the Yosemite Valley. Exhibited in New York, they brought the splendor of the Yosemite Valley to the East for the first time. These photographs were instrumental in creating political support to preserve the majestic valley and its towering sequoia trees. In June 1864, President Abraham Lincoln signed legislation that granted those lands to California to "be held for public use, resort, and recreation . . . inalienable for all time."

The Yellowstone region was little known until 1869–71 when expeditions to the area publicized their findings. Ferdinand Vandeveer Hayden led several expeditions before organizing and leading a team of scientists on a geological survey of the Yellowstone area in 1871. He invited William Henry Jackson, his photographer from the 1870 survey and recorder of frontier and Civil War life; to join the expedition along with artist Thomas Moran.

Moran had learned about the area that would become Yellowstone National Park when he illustrated an article for *Scribner's*

The Castle Geyser, Upper Geyser Basin, Yellowstone National Park Thomas Moran, artist; printed and published by Louis Prang and Co., Boston, 1874 | Chromolithograph on paper. H 41, W 51 cm | Yellowstone National Park, YELL 30

Monthly magazine titled, *"The Wonders of the Yellowstone."* Moran had accepted the magazine assignment without having seen the area. After drawing geothermal features using someone else's material, the artist looked for a way to see the area himself and joined the Hayden survey. Moran's pencil and watercolor field sketches and paintings captured the majestic landscape and documented the region's unusual terrain and natural features. About these two extraordinary artists Hayden noted, "…Mr. Jackson made the most abundant pictures. Mr. Moran was filled with enthusi-

asm and has returned to devote himself to the painting of pictures of the Yellow Stone [sic] …"

When the expedition returned, Moran's artwork was presented to members of Congress. The Federal Government purchased his massive painting, *Grand Canyon of the Yellowstone*, for the considerable sum of $10,000. It was exhibited in the U.S. Capitol in 1872. Seen by many influential politicians, this landscape painting played a critical role in fostering support for the establishment of Yellowstone National Park.

Moran's artwork and Jackson's photographs, together with Hayden's impressive findings and lobbying efforts, created support for the establishment of Yellowstone National Park in 1872. At the time of his death in 1926, Moran had painted many other areas that became national parks or monuments.

Other grand and scenic national parks such as Sequoia and Yosemite followed. There was a parallel movement to protect the prehistoric cliff dwellings, pueblos, and Spanish missions on Southwestern public lands. In 1906, President Theodore Roosevelt signed the Antiquities Act into law. The act gave the President authority to proclaim "historic landmarks, historic and prehistoric structures, and other objects of historic or scientific interest."

By 1909, when he left office, Roosevelt had proclaimed 18 national monuments, including Mesa Verde and Grand Canyon. These remarkable places inspired artists who captured their astounding beauty on canvas for all to see. By 1916, with the passage of the Organic Act, the National Park Service was authorized by Congress.

In 1917, Stephen T. Mather, the first director of the National Park Service, arranged an exhibit of American landscapes and parks by artists that included Albert Bierstadt, Thomas Moran, Carl Rungius, John Henry Twachtman, and other noted artists at the National Museum (Smithsonian Institution, National Museum of Natural History.) The exhibit was held in conjunction with the Fourth National Park Conference.

Artists' efforts to promote the splendor of the western landscape contributed to the preservation of public lands. Their landscape paintings fostered a sense of pride and identity that had helped to heal the nation after the Civil War. They also created an enduring western mystique. These landscapes and the artwork that inspired so many Americans can be enjoyed in the national parks and viewed in this volume.

With widespread support over the past century, by the National Park Service Centennial in 2016, 408 national parks were part of the National Park System.

Artists and photographers played a crucial role in preserving America's cultural and natural heritage and in the establishment of the National Park Service. Over 100 nations have been inspired by "America's best idea" to establish parks to preserve and protect their natural and cultural heritage.

National Park Service Museum Collections

"One of the most important matters to receive earnest consideration is the early establishment of adequate museums in every one of our parks ..." Stephen T. Mather, 1920

The National Park Service museum program had its origins in a modest arboretum at Yosemite in 1904. It is now one of the largest museum systems in the world. The National Park Service preserves not only places of splendor and national significance but also over 45 million objects and 76,000 linear feet of archives. The collections span the disciplines of art, archeology, archives, ethnography, history, biology, paleontology, and geology.

National Park Service Director Mather recognized the power of collections that are preserved and seen in their original context. He realized that exhibits of museum collections were a way to build public support for the national park idea. In addition to arranging an exhibit of paintings of national park scenes by well-known artists at the Smithsonian Institution in 1917, Mather also developed a traveling exhibit of photographs of park scenery that was extremely popular.

Within the year, Secretary of the Interior Franklin K. Lane established guidelines for the new National Park Service. The guidance included the statement that "... Museums containing specimens of wild flowers, shrubs, and trees, and mounted animals, birds, and fish native to the parks, and other exhibits of this character will be established as authorized."

Support for National Park Service museums increased. Universities and museums conducted research that generated some of the earliest botanical, zoological, and archeological collections for the Park Service. Historical associations assisted in developing exhibits and furnishing historic structures. In 1918, Mesa Verde exhibited prehistoric artifacts in a converted ranger cabin. In the 1920s, model park museums were developed in Yosemite, Grand Canyon, and Yellowstone National Parks. In 1933, President Franklin Roosevelt transferred historic sites (primarily American Revolution and Civil War battlefields) administered by the War Department to the National Park Service. Other parks, historic sites and national monuments, and associated collections were also transferred to National Park stewardship.

In the 1930s, National Park museums and collections benefitted from Federal projects that resulted from President Roosevelt's New Deal. The Public Works Administration funded an extension to the Mesa Verde museum and constructed many other park museums. Items created by artists and artisans in the Works Progress Administration and Civilian Conservation Corps programs were added to park collections.

Photographing The Mount of the Holy Cross William Henry Jackson, 1936 | Watercolor on artist board. H 62, W 75 cm | Scotts Bluff National Monument, SCBL 2129

In 1935, Congress passed the Historic Sites, Buildings, Objects, and Antiquities Act. The law stated that "… it is a national policy to preserve for public use historic sites, buildings, and objects of national significance for the inspiration and benefit of the people of the United States." This legislation empowered the Secretary of the Interior, working through the National Park Service, to preserve and maintain objects of national historical or archeological significance and to "establish and maintain museums in connection therewith."

By 2016, museum collections were located at over 380 National Parks throughout the United States, at six National Park Service resource centers, and over 550 non-Federal repositories. They were on view at park visitor centers, furnished historic structures, and museums. Unlike traditional museums, National Park Service collections are managed in the very places where they were gathered, recov-

(Canyon Walls) Thomas Moran, 1871 | Watercolor, gouache, and pencil on paper. H 21, W 27.5 cm
Yellowstone National Park, YELL 8543

ered, created or used. Park Service museum staff, archivists, conservators, and others document and care for the collections and make them available for research, exhibit, interpretation, education, and resource management.

National Park Service collections tell powerful stories of this land—its diverse cultures, varied habitats, flora and fauna, significant events, and innovative ideas that continue to inspire the world. Collections mirror each park's unique story and form the great National Park System mosaic. They range from everyday items that are special because they are associated with iconic American men and women, to objects of breathtaking beauty and unrivaled historical significance. Collections include flora and fauna from all corners of the land. They provide information about peoples who left no written records; reveal surprising and poignant details of Americans at home, at work, and at war; and document the rich tapestry of American habitats and ecosystems. National Park Service museum collections are an integral part of America's identity and legacy.

Scenery in the Grand Tetons Albert Bierstadt, 1865–1870 | Oil on canvas. L 75, W 111 cm | Marsh - Billings - Rockefeller National Historical Park, MABI 2843

The American Conservation Movement and the Hudson River School

"The thoroughly American branch of painting … is the landscape. It surpasses all others in popular favor, and may be said to have reached the dignity of a distinct school."

James Jackson Jarves, 1864

Landscape paintings by artists associated with the Hudson River School are particularly significant because of the School's deep associations with the American conservation movement. Before the 1820s, American artists painted portraits and documentary works depicting important historical events. Few painters attempted landscape painting.

Thomas Cole first popularized the landscape genre beginning around 1825. Views of natural wonders soon became sought after by collectors. Cole and the artists who followed his example became known as the Hudson River School. They celebrated and idealized nature above all man-made things and used allegory to express their concerns for its fragility and exploitation. Their landscapes sought to recreate the majesty and spirituality of the natural world and to inspire admiration for its beauty. Hudson River School artists' work reflected a changing attitude toward nature and the emergence of a burgeoning American conservation ethic.

After Cole's death in 1848, Asher B. Durand, an engraver and portrait painter, became the most prominent painter associated with the Hudson River School. In a series of essays entitled *Letters on Landscape Painting,* Durand set forth his idea that landscape painters should seek to depict nature exactly and not alter it in any way.

As artists celebrated nature on canvas, city dwellers who hung landscape paintings on their walls came to believe that the natural scenes depicted were worthy of preservation. At the same time, writers such as Nathaniel Hawthorne, Henry David Thoreau, and Ralph Waldo Emerson revered nature through the written word.

In the movement's later stages, artists such as Frederic Church and Albert Bierstadt expanded the ideals of the Hudson River School painters. Bierstadt captured the glowing light, luminous skies and expansive vistas of the West in his large scale canvases, including *Domes of Yosemite, In the Yosemite Valley,* and *Merced River.* Church and Bierstadt painted enormous canvases of dramatic natural scenes in the American West and around the world.

The confluence of artistic, literary, and political attention to America's scenic beauty eventually laid the foundation for the creation of the first national parks and helped establish conservation as a national value.

Artists in the Gallery and in Park Collections

Marsh - Billings - Rockefeller National Historical Park is the only national park to tell the story of conservation history and the evolving nature of land stewardship in America. Park collections include the works of some of America's finest landscape painters and members of the Hudson River School. The paintings were acquired by Frederick (1823–1890) and Julia Parmly Billings (1835–1914), and by Laurence S. Rockefeller (1910–2004) and Mary French Rockefeller (1910–1997), who was Billings' granddaughter. They are displayed in the Mansion in Woodstock, Vermont that was George Perkins Marsh's boyhood home. Marsh was one of America's first conservationists.

The Mansion was later the home of Frederick and Julia Billings, who assembled the art collection. Billings, a conservationist, pioneer in reforestation and scientific farm management, lawyer, philanthropist, and railroad builder, extended the principles of land management introduced by Marsh.

The property and collections were given to the American people in 1992 by Laurance and Mary Rockefeller. Rockefeller was a dedicated conservationist who applied the human values of stewardship to further the goals of conservation, outdoor recreation, and environmental protection in private and public arenas. He was a key supporter of the national parks.

Artwork in this gallery includes works by Albert Bierstadt, Alfred T. Bricher, Thomas Cole, Jasper F. Cropsey, Asher B. Durand, David Johnson, and John Frederick Kensett. The fine arts collection numbers over 700 and includes paintings, drawings, prints, and sculptures. *Artists represented in the collection* include Alexandre Antigna, Charles Baskerville, William Bradford, Frederic Bridgman, John W. Casilear, Harry Chase, Ruth Lambert Cheney, William Jay Dana, Harry H. Davis, Stuart E. Eldredge, Charles T. Frère, Sanford Robinson Gifford, Adele Herter, Hermann Herzog, Kaoru Kawano, William Keith, Frances Johnson Kidder, Edward Moran, Peter Moran, Anna Mary Robertson "Grandma" Moses, W. Percy Richardson, Jay Robinson, Sanford Ross, Thomas Prichard Rossiter, George Henry Smillie, Hiroshige Utagawa, Frank Waller, Arthur Bricket Wilder, Thomas Waterman Wood, Alice Geddes Woodward, Laura Woodward, and others.

Longfellow House - Washington's Headquarters National Historic Site artwork in this gallery is by John Frederick Kensett and Albert Bierstadt. See the *Eminent Americans at Home* gallery for information on artists represented in the collection.

San Francisco Maritime National Historical Park artwork in this gallery is by Elizabeth A. Rockwell. See the *Eminent Americans at Home* gallery for information on artists represented in the collection.

Thomas Edison National Historical Park artwork in this gallery is by Sanford Robinson Gifford. See the *Eminent Americans at Home* gallery for information on artists represented in the collection.

Cathedral Rocks, Yosemite Albert Bierstadt, 1870 | Oil on panel. L 60, W 45 cm
Marsh - Billings - Rockefeller National Historical Park, MABI 4162

Study, Harbor Island, Lake George David Johnson, 1871 | Oil on canvas. L 34, W 59.67 cm
Marsh - Billings - Rockefeller National Historical Park, MABI 1592

(Waterfall) John Frederick Kensett, ca. 1856 | Oil on canvas. H 37.8, W 31.4 cm
Longfellow House - Washington's Headquarters National Historic Site, LONG 4135

High Bridge, New York
Jasper Francis Cropsey
1879
Oil on canvas. L 29.5, W 60.5 cm
Marsh - Billings - Rockefeller
National Historical Park, MABI 3801

Tower by Moonlight
Thomas Cole
ca. 1838
Oil on panel. L 24, W 35.5 cm
Marsh - Billings - Rockefeller
National Historical Park, MABI 4423

The Hudson River Elizabeth A. Rockwell, ca. 1878 | Oil on sheet steel and masonite. H 42, W 130 cm
San Francisco Maritime National Historical Park, SAFR 3774

On the Beach Sanford Robinson Gifford, ca. 1870 | Oil on canvas. L 22.9, W 45.8 cm | Thomas Edison National Historical Park, EDIS 102274

Golden October
Alfred T. Bricher
1870
Oil on canvas. L 60, W 50 cm
Marsh - Billings - Rockefeller
National Historical Park, MABI 2815

Lake George at Sunset
John Frederick Kensett
1872
Oil on canvas. L 59.5, W 90.5 cm
Marsh - Billings - Rockefeller
National Historical Park, MABI 2814

Departure of Hiawatha
Albert Bierstadt
1868
Oil on canvas. H 40.3, W 46.3 cm
Longfellow House - Washington's Headquarters
National Historic Site, LONG 4138

Autumn Landscape
Asher B. Durand
ca. 1847
Oil on canvas. L 29, W 41.5 cm
Marsh - Billings - Rockefeller
National Historical Park, MABI 2813

Niagara Falls
Thomas Cole
1829–1830
Oil on wood panel. L 46, W 60 cm
Marsh - Billings - Rockefeller
National Historical Park, MABI 1770

Sunset in the Yosemite Valley William Bradford, 1881 | Oil on canvas. L 69.5, W 120.5 cm | Marsh - Billings - Rockefeller National Historical Park, MABI 1758

America's Treasured Places

America's Treasured Places

"Then it seemed to me the Sierra should be called ... the Range of Light ... the most divinely beautiful of all the mountain chains I have ever seen." John Muir

American landscape paintings in National Park Service collections capture the beauty of the nation's diverse regions. Western artwork portrays magnificent and rugged mountains, towering sequoias, arid plains studded with piñon trees and silver sagebrush, and shimmering hot deserts. Lakes, waterfalls, and dense forests are featured in Northeastern landscapes. Habitats vary from lushly tropical to dramatic natural phenomena.

Landscape art in America was popularized from the early nineteenth century, just as a young nation began to explore its expansive and varying geography and its relationship to the land. Many artists traveled beyond the Rocky Mountains to experience America's natural splendors. They sought to capture the drama and beauty of the West.

For some, western expansion fulfilled America's Manifest Destiny as railroads expanded to accommodate exploration, tourism, and settlement. For others, this expansion raised concerns for the displacement of Native Americans and the exploitation of natural resources.

The monumental scenery represented in American landscape paintings helped establish conservation as a national value. The Yosemite Valley and the wonders of Yellowstone inspired national leaders to protect and preserve special places for the benefit and appreciation of America's citizens, present and future.

The artists who captured these magnificent landscapes contributed to the formation of the National Park Service that protects and preserves the nation's most beautiful and significant places.

People's fascination with these places endures because of their power, beauty, and representation of the nation's identity. These artworks embody the very landscapes that are preserved and protected in America's national parks.

(W. Spring C. July 8, Idaho) Thomas Moran, 1871
Watercolor, gouache, and pencil on paper. H 8, W 17.5 cm
Yellowstone National Park, YELL 8535

Artists in the Gallery and in Park Collections

Bandelier National Monument collections relate to the over 11,000 year human presence in the canyons and mesas of the Pajarito Plateau. This gallery includes artwork by Helmut Naumer, Sr., who created pastels of park scenes and nearby pueblos.

Big Cypress National Preserve collections relate to the subtropical wilderness and marine estuaries in southern Florida and include artwork by Sam Vinikoff. *Artists represented in the collection* include Mark Fletcher, Damien Joseph, Jacqueline Roch, and others.

Carlsbad Caverns National Park collections relate to the geological and biological specimens collected from caves. This gallery includes artwork by William Howard Shuster.

Crater Lake National Park collections relate to the park's deep blue lake, surrounding high cliffs, and its violent volcanic past. This gallery includes paintings by Paul Clark Rockwood that document phases of Mount Mazama's eruption. *Artists represented in the collection* include Eugene Kingman, Chris (Christian) Jorgensen, Craig Thomas, Gunnar Widforss, and others.

Death Valley National Park collections relate to the below-sea-level basin and the land of extremes. This gallery includes artwork by Calhoun Collins, John Hilton, and Robert Francis Williams. *Artists represented in the collection* are Kathi Hilton, Chris Jorgenson, Edward Langley, Mary Liddecoat, Sylvia McGee, David Neufeld, Bill Radcliff, Helen Robertson, Paul H. Webber, Jr., and others. Spanish Colonial Revival and California Mission decorative arts and furnishings are on view in Scotty's Castle, located in Grapevine Canyon 3,000 feet above the desert floor.

Everglades National Park collections relate to the subtropical wilderness and marine estuaries in southern Florida and include artwork by Walter Alois Weber. *Artists represented in the collection* include Thomas P. Bernard, Richard F. Deckert, Edward J. Glannon, Charley Harper, Helga Raftery, and others.

Grand Canyon National Park collections document early explorers and miners, the modern tourism industry, and the archeology and natural history of the park. Artwork in this gallery is by Thomas Moran, Charles Dorman Robinson, and Gunnar Widforss. *Artists represented in the collection* include Mary Ogden Abbott, Kevin Adams, Karen Ahlgren, Bruce Aiken, Roy Andersen, Jules Baumann, Carl Oscar Borg, Ferdinand Burgdorff, Howard Russell Butler, Jennifer Sullivan Carney, John D. Cogan, Arthur E. Demaray, Lorna M. Durfey, Hurlstone Fairchild, Gene Foster, Robert Goldman, Carl Hoermann, Chris Jorgensen, Fred Kabotie, Robert E. Smith, and others.

Hawai'i Volcanoes National Park fine arts collections depict the island's tropical beauty and natural phenomena. Artwork in this gallery is by D. Howard Hitchcock and Lloyd Sexton, Jr. *Artists represented in the collection* include Donald M. Black, Charles Furneaux, William Hartman, H. Kawainui Kane, Wesley Kanetake, Paul Martin, Ann Rathbun, Paul Rockwood, Jules Tavernier, William Twigg-Smith, Lionel Walden, and others.

Jefferson National Expansion Memorial collections document St. Louis' role in the Westward Expansion of the United States during the nineteenth century. Artwork in this gallery is by Thomas Moran. *Artists represented in the collection* include Carl Bodmer, Oscar Berninghaus, Lee Brubaker, Leon De Pomarede, Stanley Del, Ferdinand

V. Hayden, Benno Jansenn, Joseph John Jones, William Macy, Beaman Meacham, Charles A. Morgenthaler, James Mulcahy, Joseph Pennell, Fernand Quesne, Siegfried Reinhardt, Paul Rockwood, and others.

Marsh - Billings - Rockefeller National Historical Park artwork in this gallery is by D. Howard Hitchcock and William Bradford. See *The American Conservation Movement and the Hudson River School* gallery for artists represented in the collection.

National Park Service, Museum Management Program artwork in this gallery is by Eugene Kingman and Walter Alois Weber.

Sagamore Hill National Historic Site collections relate to President Theodore Roosevelt at Sagamore Hill, his home in Oyster Bay, New York that served as the "Summer White House" from 1902 to 1908. This gallery includes work by Lucien Whiting Powell. *Artists represented in the collection* include Carter J. Beard, Francis Soule Campbell, John Carlin, Howard Christy, W.B. Closson, Adrian De Groot, Alexander Drysdale, Albrecht Durer, Fedor Encke, Daniel Huntingdon, Mabel La Farge, Julian Lamar, Pinckney Marcius-Simons, Frederic Remington, Carl Rungius, Augustus Saint-Gaudens, Marcus P. Simons, Jay W. Weaver, and others.

Scotts Bluff National Monument collections focus on the history of the Oregon Trail and include photographs, sketches, and watercolors by William Henry Jackson, photographer, artist, and member of the Hayden Geological Expedition of 1871.

Yellowstone National Park collections document the cultural and natural history of the Yellowstone region. They include accounts of early pioneer experiences in the park, historic photographs, and works of art depicting Yellowstone's natural beauty. Artwork in this gallery includes Thomas Moran's field sketches, watercolors, chromolithographs, and oil paintings. *Artists represented in the collection* are Charles Livingston Bull, William Chapman, Henry Wood Elliot, William Henry Holmes, William Henry Jackson, Charles Moore, James Everett Stuart, Walter Trumbull, John Henry Twachtman, Robert F. Williams, and others.

Yosemite National Park collections document the cultural and natural history of the Yosemite region and include historic photographs and ethnographic materials such as basketry, dance regalia, featherwork, and beadwork from the area. Artwork in this gallery is by Mary Muir Hand, Thomas Hill, William Keith, Thomas Moran, Chiura Obata, Charles Dorman Robinson, and Gunnar Widforss. *Artists represented in the collection* include Thomas Almond Ayres, George Baker, Harry Cassie Best, Albert Bierstadt, William Bradford, Ferdinand Burgdorff, Constance Gordon Cumming, Jane Culp, Edwin Deakin, George Fiske, Mary V. Hood, Chris Jorgensen, Thomas Laycock, Gustave F. Liljestrom, Mary Nimmo Moran, Andreas Roth, Sandra Rouverol, Frederick Ferdinand Schafer, Benjamin Willard Sears, James Smillie, Robert Williams, Theodore Wores, Hiroshi Yoshida, and others.

Zion National Park collections document the massive canyon where ancient native peoples and pioneers traveled. This gallery includes artwork by Howard Russell Butler and Frederick S. Dellenbaugh. *Artists represented in the collection* include Lynn Berryhill, William Henry Jackson, William H. Wagoner, and others.

Hot Springs of Gardiner's River, Yellowstone Park Thomas Moran, 1871 | Watercolor, gouache, and pencil on paper. H 25, W 33 cm
Yellowstone National Park, YELL 8529

Tower Falls and Sulphur Mountain - Yellowstone Thomas Moran, artist; published and printed by Louis Prang and Co., Boston, 1874
Chromolithograph on paper. H 41, W 51 cm | Yellowstone National Park, YELL 21

The American West

"It was during one of the darkest hours, before Sherman had begun the march upon Atlanta or Grant his terrible movement through the Wilderness, when the paintings of Bierstadt and the photographs of Watkins, both productions of the War time, had given to the people on the Atlantic some idea of the sublimity of the Yosemite ..." Frederick Law Olmsted, 1864

Artists of the nineteenth century played a key role in helping to heal the nation following the Civil War. Beginning with pioneering photographer Carleton Watkins (1829–1916) and his impressive portfolio of Western landscape prints, many artists provided visual evidence of the majesty of the American West. Most Americans could not imagine the drama of western landscapes until artists like Thomas Moran and Albert Bierstadt, inspired by Watkins, traveled west and documented the grand vistas on canvas.

These artists made the panoramic landscapes and natural phenomena of the West accessible to the general public. Moran's extraordinary artwork captured Yellowstone's unusual terrain and natural features. A skilled illustrator and an admirer of English artist John M. W. Turner, Moran also painted several areas that later became national parks, including the Grand Canyon.

On returning home, some artists took their paintings on tour, charging admission to see the painted wonders of the West. Most who came to see the paintings had not traveled west and were amazed by what they saw. These works of art shaped how viewers perceived these magnificent scenes and fostered the movement to conserve the natural world.

The monumental Western landscape paintings, sketches, and photography were displayed in the halls of Congress. They played a crucial role in the passage of a law requiring that the Yosemite Valley be set aside and protected for the future enjoyment of all citizens. In 1872, Yellowstone became the first national park, signifying a commitment to conservation stewardship as a national value.

Artists of the late nineteenth and early twentieth centuries captured Western vistas that ranged from the rugged mountains and deep valleys of the high Sierras to the below-sea-level deserts of California and the awe-inspiring Grand Canyon.

The sweeping landscapes of the Four Corners—Arizona, New Mexico, Colorado and Utah—were alluring to painters and photographers alike. They recognized the remarkable quality of the Southwestern light that rendered the landscape and distant horizons distinctly. Artists, many from Eastern cities, were drawn to the engaging confluence of cultures and the vast light filled terrain. Their canvases framed the big skies, mesas, and canyons and distilled its radiant beauty, intense color, and majestic grandeur.

The Mountain of the Holy Cross, Colorado Thomas Moran, artist; printed and published by Louis Prang and Co., Boston, 1876 | Chromolithograph on paper. H 41, W 51 cm
Yellowstone National Park, YELL 26

Shiva's Temple
Thomas Moran
1892
Watercolor on paper. L 19.8, W 11.9 cm
Jefferson National Expansion Memorial, JEFF 4296

The Devil Tower
Thomas Moran
1892
Pencil on paper. L 17.5, W 11.2 cm
Jefferson National Expansion Memorial, JEFF 4222

Tower Creek
Thomas Moran
1871
Watercolor on paper. H 19.7, W 26.8 cm
Yellowstone National Park, YELL 8528

Yellowstone National Park, Wyoming Eugene Kingman, ca. 1930s | Oil on canvas. L 89, W 110 cm
National Park Service, Museum Management Program, WASOA 45

15 Parley's Canon - Lower Part
William Henry Jackson
ca. 1866
Watercolor on artist board. H 14, W 21.5 cm
Scotts Bluff National Monument, SCBL 127

Chimney Rock, July 31, 1866
William Henry Jackson
1866
Watercolor on paper. H 8, W 13 cm
Scotts Bluff National Monument, SCBL 24

Bridalveil Fall Thomas Moran, ca. 1924 | Oil on canvas. H 89.5, W 63.5 cm
Yosemite National Park, YOSE 57883

(View from Inspiration Point) Thomas Hill, ca. 1885 | Oil on canvas. H 87, W 71.8 cm | Yosemite National Park, YOSE 49909

(Yosemite Valley from Inspiration Point)
William Keith
ca. 1880s
Oil on canvas. L 63.5, W 44.5 cm
Yosemite National Park, YOSE 10575

The Two Regalities
Charles Dorman Robinson
After 1880
Oil on canvas. L 80, W 60.3 cm
Yosemite National Park, YOSE 13558

Winter Evening in Yosemite Valley Gunnar Widforss, 1923 | Watercolor on paper. H 40.2, W 48.3 cm | Yosemite National Park, YOSE 90228

El Capitan; Yosemite National Park U.S.A. Chiura Obata, ca. 1930
Woodblock print on paper. H 53.2, W 41.6 cm | Yosemite National Park, YOSE 109528

(Cathedral Spires)
Mary Muir Hand
ca. 1897
Oil on canvas. L 76.2, W 61 cm
Yosemite National Park, YOSE 25527

Sequoia National Park, California
Eugene Kingman
ca. 1930s
Oil on canvas. L 165.5, W 89.6 cm
National Park Service,
Museum Management Program, WASOA 47

(View from the South Rim of Inner Canyon) Gunnar Widforss, Early 1900s | Watercolor on paper.
H 36, W 45.9 cm | Grand Canyon National Park, GRCA 51205

Evening, Grand Canyon Lucien Whiting Powell, Late 1890s–early 1900s | Oil on canvas, H 58.4, W 94 cm
Sagamore Hill National Historic Site, SAHI 545

(Grand Canyon from the North Rim)
Charles Dorman Robinson
1929
Oil on canvas. W 122, H 93 cm
Grand Canyon National Park, GRCA 13669

(View of the Grand Canyon from the Rim)
Thomas Moran
1911
Oil on canvas. W 28.5, H 17.3 cm
Grand Canyon National Park, GRCA 13629

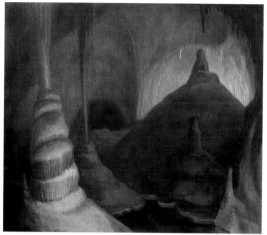

Dome Room
William Howard Shuster
1924
Oil on canvas. L 101.6, W 121.9 cm
Carlsbad Caverns National Park, CAVE 2659

Green Lake
William Howard Shuster
1924
Oil on canvas. L 91.4, W 121.9 cm
Carlsbad Caverns National Park, CAVE 2661

Zion Canyon
Frederick Samuel Dellenbaugh
1903
Oil on canvas. W 95.9, H 63.2 cm
Zion National Park, ZION 38105

Mountains of the Sun
Howard Russell Butler
1926
Oil on canvas. W 165.1, H 139.7 cm
Zion National Park, ZION 14586

Late Afternoon in Zion Canyon Howard Russell Butler, 1926 | Oil on canvas. W 412, H 116.8 cm
Zion National Park, ZION 14581

Sand Dunes of Death Valley
Calhoun (Cal) Collins
1954
Paint and ground stone on glass. W 55.8, H 42.1 cm
Death Valley National Park, DEVA 4876

Breakfast Canyon
Robert Francis Williams
ca. 1950s
Oil on canvas. W 121.9, H 91.4 cm
Death Valley National Park, DEVA 2059

Desert Sprint John Hilton, ca. 1950s | Oil on canvas. W 106.6, H 81.3 cm | Death Valley National Park, DEVA 3300

Mount Mazama Under Maximum Glaciation (1 of 3)
Paul Clark Rockwood
ca. 1939
Oil on canvas-on-masonite. H 52.9 cm, W 75.6 cm
Crater Lake National Park, CRLA 846B

Mount Mazama Before Collapse (2 of 3)
Paul Clark Rockwood
ca. 1939
Oil on masonite. H 52.9, W 75.6 cm
Crater Lake National Park, CRLA 846A

**Mount Mazama After the Cataclysmic
Eruption (3 of 3)**
Paul Clark Rockwood
ca. 1939
Oil on masonite. H 52.9, W 75.6 cm
Crater Lake National Park, CRLA 847

Crater Lake National Park Eugene Kingman, ca. 1930s | Oil on canvas. L 110.8, W 90.7 cm
National Park Service, Museum Management Program, WASOA 48

Administration Building, Frijoles Canyon
Helmut Naumer Sr.
1935–1936
Pastel on paper. H 30.5, L 47 cm
Bandelier National Monument, BAND 1409

Picuris Pueblo
Helmut Naumer Sr.
1935–1936
Pastel on paper. H 30.5, L 47 cm
Bandelier National Monument, BAND 1410

Frijoles Canyon, Second View
Helmut Naumer Sr.
1935–1936
Pastel on paper. H 48.7, L 33.5 cm, framed.
Bandelier National Monument, BAND 1406

View of Talus House
Helmut Naumer Sr.
1935–1936
Pastel on paper. H 55, L 70 cm
Bandelier National Monument, BAND 1437

'Ohi'a Lehua Lloyd Sexton, Jr., 1946 | Oil on canvas. H 61, W 76.2 cm | Hawai'i Volcanoes National Park, HAVO 8

Views of Paradise

"… We rejoice that (the artist), has become so charmed with the contemplation of the scenery, that he is endeavouring to transfer some of its beauties to the canvas…"

Reverend S.C. Damon, Seaman's Chaplain of Honolulu, 1867

Tropical landscapes are among the rarest of American landscapes. Many plants and animal species found their way across the Pacific to produce a unique and complex Hawaiian ecosystem. Marshes, swamps, tropical forests and waterfalls, as well as coastal dunes and fiery volcanoes, have long been alluring to artists who sought to capture the spectacular and unfamiliar beauty of these special places. The endless beaches and shallow lagoons of glinting water, fertile lands bound by fronded palm trees, and unusual and vibrantly colored flora were inspirational.

Eruptions of Kilauea and Mauna Loa produced fiery fountains and rivers of molten lava that, over time, created a volcanic landscape. An art movement known as the Volcano School (1880–1890) emerged in response to the growing interest in documenting the dramatic natural occurrences of volcanic eruptions that were frequent during this period. Many of the painters of the Volcano School painted other Hawaiian subjects, including landscapes of the island. Sketches and paintings of volcanic eruptions were extremely popular and highly collectible. They also did much to enhance tourism to the island.

Florida's varied habitats, meanwhile, include mangrove swamps and rich marine estuaries that support an abundant diversity of wildlife. The wildlife artist captured the alligator lying still in the intense heat of the humid day. Bright and closely observed birds on land and in flight against the intense aquamarine and cobalt skies are framed by tropical vegetation. Water is ever present in the depictions of the grey-green wetlands, creeks, and backwaters of the mangrove swamps.

These magnificent views of paradise are preserved and protected by the National Park Service and continue to inspire artists and visitors.

(Lava overflowing from Halema'uma'u Crater onto the floor of Kilauea Caldera) D. Howard Hitchcock, 1894
Oil on canvas. H 69, W 109.2 cm | Hawai'i Volcanoes National Park, HAVO 452

Dana Lake D. Howard Hitchcock, 1894 | Oil on canvas. H 49.5, W 106.7 cm | Hawai'i Volcanoes National Park, HAVO 804

Moku'aweoweo D. Howard Hitchcock, 1896 | Oil on canvas. H 53.3, W 101.6 | Hawai'i Volcanoes National Park, HAVO 451

Mauna Kea D. Howard Hitchcock, 1888 | Oil on canvas. L 30, W 76 cm | Marsh - Billings - Rockefeller National Historical Park, MABI 2842

American Crocodile
Walter Alois Weber
ca. 1930s
Oil on canvas. H 51, W 68.5 cm
Everglades National Park, EVER 7005

Hidden Lake
Sam Vinikoff
1998
Oil on canvas. H 76.2, W 101.6 cm
Big Cypress National Preserve, BICY 14613

Nene
Walter Alois Weber
Late 1930s
Oil on canvas. L 81.5, W 61 cm
National Park Service,
Museum Management Program, WASOA 39

Puerto Rican Parrots
Walter Alois Weber
Late 1930s
Oil on canvas. W 60, L 44.5 cm
National Park Service,
Museum Management Program, WASOA 7

Roseate Spoonbills Walter Alois Weber, Late 1930s | Oil on canvas. L 101.6, W 56 cm
National Park Service, Museum Management Program, WASOA 43

Braintree Samuel Malcolm, 1798 | Watercolor on paper. H 30.5, W 43 cm | Adams National Historical Park, ADAM 182

Eminent Americans at Home

Eminent Americans at Home

"The greatest thing I have learned is how good it is to come home again." Eleanor Roosevelt

Homes are private spaces that reflect personal style and taste. They showcase interests and life experiences. Each home contains its own story and provides a view into the life and times of its inhabitants.

For well-known Americans of the late nineteenth and early twentieth centuries, their homes, often grand structures filled with elegant possessions, reflected their fame and prosperity. Fine art on display in the home had decorative merit and discreetly communicated values, as well as economic and social status.

Rustic pastoral landscapes often decorated dining rooms and parlors. Maritime scenes filled with sailing vessels and scenes of rivers and lakes were extremely popular. Many were displayed in formal parlors and in summer homes. European works of art that were collected on trips abroad served as a record of places that had been visited by affluent families on the Grand Tour.

Homeowners delighted in surrounding themselves with landscapes that were inspired by America's natural beauty. These works of art also reflected the collectors' patriotism and growing support of the American conservation movement. Others displayed charming views of their homes that brought joy and a sense of pride and continuity.

While eminent Americans had a public life and persona, it was in the privacy of their own homes that they experienced some of the most memorable and cherished moments of their lives. The home provided a comforting retreat from the pressures of public life. It was a place where they were surrounded by family and where they could relax and enjoy the comfort of familiar furnishings and works of art.

The artworks in this gallery offer an entry into the private world and home life of distinguished public figures who have had a profound impact on the nation and contributed to shaping America's history and identity. Included are Presidents and first ladies, Revolutionary and Civil War generals, inventors, artists, ranchers, writers, and many others honored by the nation.

These works of art are preserved by the National Park Service and can be seen in their original settings within the homes of these distinguished Americans. They provide a rare, intimate, and evocative glimpse of domestic life at home, with the family, and at leisure.

Artists in the Gallery and in Park Collections

Adams National Historical Park collections relate to the Old House, the Adams Family Mansion, ca. 1730, the birthplace of two presidents; John Adams (1797–1801) and John Quincy Adams (1825–1829), and home to Congressman Charles Francis Adams and historian Henry Adams. Artwork in this gallery is by Godfrey N. Frankenstein and Samuel Malcolm. *Artists represented in the collection* include Mather Brown, Alfred Quinton Collins, Chester Harding, Edward Harris, William Morris Hunt, Charles Bird King, Edward Marchant, Frank D. Millet, Charles Wilson Peale, Samuel Worchester Rouse, Edward Savage, Jane Stuart — after Gilbert Stuart, Frederick P. Vinton, William Edward West, William Joseph Williams, William Winstanley, Joseph Wood, and others.

Arlington House, the Robert E. Lee National Memorial collections relate to three of Virginia's most influential families: the Washingtons, Custises, and Lees. Artwork in in this gallery is by Benson J. Lossing and Elizabeth Moore Reid. *Artists represented in the collection* include George Washington Parke Custis, Mary Custis Lee, John Wollaston's portrait of Martha Washington hand-colored by Mrs. Robert E. Lee, Mathilde M. Leisenring, Margaret Loughborough, Charly Miyan, William D. Washington, William G. Williams, Martha (Markie) Custis Williams, and others.

Carl Sandburg National Historic Site collections relate to "Poet of the People" and Lincoln biographer, Carl Sandburg, his wife Mrs. Paula Steichen Sandburg, and their family at Connemara farm in Flat Rock, North Carolina. Artwork in this gallery is by Katsushika Hokusai. *Artists represented in the collection* include Thomas Hart Benton, Alexander Calder, Jan Clausing, Helga Sandburg, Margaret Sandburg, Bette Anne Wilkie, and others.

Clara Barton National Historic Site collections relate to Clara Barton, founder of the American Red Cross, at her Glen Echo, Maryland home that served as the first headquarters of the Red Cross. Artwork in this gallery is attributed to Ms. Barton and believed to have been made during her stay in Europe.

Cumberland Island National Seashore collections relate to the Carnegie family's winter retreat on Plum Orchard Mansion on the island from 1908–1972. Artwork in this gallery is by Thomas Bigelow Craig, Peter Possart, and Theodore Alexander Weber. *Artists represented in the collection* include Carlton T. Chapman, Charles P. Gruppé, Berger Listen, Della Rischarde, A. Bryan Wall, and others.

Eisenhower National Historic Site collections relate to President Dwight D. Eisenhower and Mrs. Mamie Eisenhower at their home and weekend retreat at Gettysburg Farm, Pennsylvania. This gallery includes a landscape painted by President Eisenhower in 1955 while he was recovering at Fitzsimmons Army Hospital from his first heart attack. *Artists represented in the collection* include George M. Cochran, Elizabeth Draper, Helen Janet Knief, Arthur Sasse, Thomas E. Stephens, Ramona Winchell, and others.

Frederick Douglass National Historic Site collections relate to abolitionist Frederick Douglass and Cedar Hill, his home in Anacostia, Washington, DC where he lived from 1878 until his death in 1895. Artwork in this gallery is by Edmund Clarence Messer. *Artists represented in the collection* include J. E. Baker, C. Becker, Joseph Coormans, Sara J. Eddy, Leopold Grozelier, John H. Littlefield, Gerrit Smith Loguen, James E. Taylor, John R. White, and others.

Grant-Kohrs Ranch National Historic Site collections relate to cattle ranching in the American West from the 1850s to the 1980s and the day-to-day management of livestock at the Deer Lodge, Montana ranch. *Artists represented in the collection* include Edwin William Bache, J. H. Bufford, Nina Johnson, William Kruse Kohrs, Bonnie Maisons, John T. Mason, Bartolome Esteban Murillo Rigal, Vern H. Ruttenbur, Louis P. Thompson, and Patricia Nell Warren.

Hampton National Historical Site collections relate to Mid-Atlantic life from before the American Revolution to after World War II. Artists in this gallery are John Carlin, Michele Pagano, and Helen West Stewart Ridgely. *Artists represented in the collection* include William Russell Birch, John Hesselius, William James Hubard, John Wesley Jarvis, Florence Maccubbin, Charles Wilson Peale, James Peale, Rembrandt Peale, Bass Otis, John E. Robertson, George L. Saunders, Thomas Sully, Philip Tilyard, Camillo de Vito, Charles Volkmar, Jr., Charles Volkmar, Sr., and Thomas B. Welch.

Harry S Truman National Historic Site collections relate to President Harry S Truman and Mrs. Bess Wallace Truman in their Independence, Missouri home that was known as the "Summer White House" from 1945 to 1952. Artwork in this gallery is by Wallace Nutting. *Artists represented in the collection* include Thomas Hart Benton, Neal Butcher, Oliver J. Corbett, A. F. Duggan, Jay Wesley Jacobs, Greta Kempton, Leroy Daniel Macmoriss, Ron Marsh, Matthew A. Monks, Glenn Murray, Ruth Norris, Franz Papez, Grace E. Taylor, Robert Tindall, Frederick Judd Waugh, and others.

Home of Franklin D. Roosevelt National Historic Site collections relate to Springwood, the estate in Hyde Park, New York that President Roosevelt loved and considered home. Artwork in this gallery is by Albert Henry Munsell. *Artists represented in the collection* are William Adolphe Bouguereau, Daniel Huntington (attrib), Henry Inman, Eastman Johnson, Leonard Howard Reedy, Adolf Schreyer, Gilbert Stuart (attrib), Prince Pierre Troubetkoy, Ross Turner, Julian Alden Weir, and others.

Jimmy Carter National Historic Site collections relate to President Jimmy Carter and Mrs. Rosalynn Carter in their Plains, Georgia home. Artwork in this gallery includes a watercolor by Kenneth P. Craig.

Lincoln Home National Historic Site collections relate to President Abraham Lincoln and Mrs. Mary Todd Lincoln and family in their Springfield, Illinois home. Work in this gallery is from *Harper's Weekly*.

Longfellow House - Washington's Headquarters National Historic Site collections relate to Henry Wadsworth Longfellow's home that had served as General George Washington's headquarters during the Siege of Boston, July 1775–April 1776. The collection includes over 1800 paintings, drawings, prints, and sculptures. Artists in this gallery are George Loring Brown, John Baptiste Camille Corot, John Enneking, Myles Birket Foster, Theodore Gudin, Eugène Louis Gabriel Isabey, Ernest Wadsworth Longfellow, and Nicolai Martin Ulfsten. *Artists represented in the collection* include Francis Alexander, Washington Allston, Lorenzo Bartolini, Albert Bierstadt, J. Appleton Brown, Mather Brown, Benjamin Champney, John Gadsby Chapman, Thomas Crawford, Daniel de Blieck, Florence Freeman, Winckworth Allan Gay, George Healy, William Morris Hunt, Eastman Johnson, John Kensett, Anna Klumpke, Rose Lamb, Pierre Jules Mene, Friedrick Overbeck, Samuel Prout, Ellen Robbins, Gilbert Stuart, and others.

Marsh - Billings - Rockefeller National Historic Site artwork in this gallery is by Albert Bierstadt and Edward Moran. See *The American Conservation Movement and the Hudson River School* gallery for information on the artists in the collection.

Morristown National Historical Park collections commemorate the sites of General Washington and the Continental Army's winter encampment of December 1779 through June 1780. Artwork in this gallery is by Edward Kranich. *Artists represented in the collection* include Gainsborough Dupont, Herman Gustave Herkomer, Henry Inman, Charles Mackubin Lefferts, Raphaelle Peale,

Rembrandt Peale, Frederick B. Revere (attrib), Edward Savage, Joseph Scheverle, Julian Scott, Gilbert Stuart, Jane Stuart (attrib), Thomas Sully, and others.

National Park Service, Museum Management Program artwork in this gallery includes work by Thomas Moran.

Sagamore Hill National Historic Site collections relate to President Theodore Roosevelt at Sagamore Hill, his home in Oyster Bay, New York that served as the "Summer White House" from 1902 to 1908. Artwork in this gallery is by Pinckney Marcius-Simons. See the *America's Treasured Places* gallery for artists in the collection.

Saint-Gaudens National Historic Site collections relate to sculptor Augustus Saint-Gaudens and his work, home, and studios in Cornish, New Hampshire. Artists in this gallery are George de Forest Brush and Augusta Fisher Homer Saint-Gaudens, the sculptor's wife. *Artists represented in the collection* include Elmer Wood Bartlett, Winston Churchill, Kenyon Cox, Thomas Wilmer Dewing, Barry Faulkner, Mary Foote, Eisen Kikukawa, Charles A. Platt, Annetta J. Saint-Gaudens, Augustus Saint-Gaudens, Carlota Saint-Gaudens, Louis Saint-Gaudens, Frances C. Houston, William Henry Hyde, John La Farge, Arvia Mackaye, Naomi Rhodes, Stephen Parrish, Abbott Thayer, Hiroshige Utagawa, Jean-Antoine Watteau, Stanford White, and others.

San Francisco Maritime National Historical Park collections relate to the maritime history of the Pacific Coast and the San Francisco Bay area from the mid-19th century to the present. Artists in this gallery are Thomas Colb and Chris (Christian) Jorgensen. *Artists represented in the collection* include Woolston Barratt, Henry Bernahl, Reginald Arthur Borstel, Oswald Brett, William A. Coulter, Gideon Jacques Denny, Herman Dietz, William Edgar, William Gilkerson, Gordon Grant, Arthur Victor Gregory, George Frederick Gregory, Takuya Hagiwara, Antonio Jacobsen, Louis Macouillard, Darrell McClure, Mark Richard Myers, Otis Oldfield, Dorothy Puccinelli, John Milton Ramm, Charles Dorman Robinson, H. Shimidzu, Eric Tufnell, William Howard Yorke, and others.

Thomas Edison National Historical Park collections relate to inventor Thomas Edison, his New Jersey Laboratory complex, and his home, Glenmont, where he lived for over 45 years. Artists in this gallery are Charles Henry Ebert, William Hart, Henry Hudson Holly, Frances W. Horne, Jonathan Bradley Morse, and Samuel Peter Rolt Triscott. *Artists represented in the collection* include Abraham Archibald Anderson, Hilda Belcher, Rosa Bonheur, Alexander Cabanel, Louis Douzette, George P. Fayko, Herman Geyer, Sanford Robinson Gifford, Lucius Wolcott Hitchcock, Gustave Kruell, Jean Paul Lelinger, Maximilian Rapine, Guido Reni, Paul Seignac, Ellis M. Silvette, Domenico Tojetti, Eugene Verboeckhoven, Dorothy E. Vicaji, and others.

Tuskegee Institute National Historic Site collections relate to Booker T. Washington, George Washington Carver, and the Tuskegee Institute. Artwork in this gallery is by George Washington Carver, who rose from slavery to become a renowned educator, naturalist, and artist.

Vanderbilt Mansion National Historic Site collections relate to the Gilded Age country estate at Hyde Park, New York that illustrates economic, social, cultural, and demographic changes that occurred as America industrialized after the Civil War. Artists in this gallery are Johann Hermann Carmiencke, Edmund Darch Lewis, and Frank Chickering Warren. *Artists represented in the collection* include William Adolphe Bouguereau and Adolf Schreyer.

Weir Farm National Historic Site collections relate to American Impressionist Julian Alden Weir and other artists who designed and preserved Weir Farm in Connecticut as a setting of artistic expression. Artwork in this gallery is by Julian Alden Weir. *Artists represented in the collection* include Olin Warner, Irene Weir, Robert Walter Weir, Dorothy Weir Young, Mahonri M. Young, and others.

Arlington House Benson J. Lossing, 1853 | Paper, watercolor. L 21, W 24 cm | Arlington House, The Robert E. Lee Memorial, ARHO 123

Views of Home

"I think to christen my place by the name of Peace field, in commemoration of the peace which I assisted in making in 1783, of the thirteen years peace and neutrality which I have contributed to preserve and of the constant peace and tranquility which I have enjoyed in this residence." John Adams, 1796

Artworks that depict homes provide an enchanting visual record. They record details of architecture and craftsmanship. Paintings and sketches document the built environment of the period. They capture the personality and charm of the home, from rustic wooden cabin, to ranch house, to elegant mansion. They provide engaging portraits of historic homes surrounded by gardens, on town streets, and on country roads. These artworks enable us to place their occupants within the context of the cultural landscape of their lives and times.

Artworks that depict views of much loved residences provide a sense of continuity and confidence to the following generations who will also occupy the home. They provide the owners with a fond remembrance of family life. Diplomat Henry White (1850–1927), son of Eliza "Didy" Ridgely of Hampton and grandson of Eliza Ridgely, made the following comment about his beloved Hampton, "By far the happiest recollections of my childhood… were long annual sojourns … at Hampton. The older I become, the more do I realize how valuable a background to a man in after life is the country home of his childhood … At most of the interesting periods … of my public life, my memory has harked back to … the early days at Hampton …"

The National Park Service pays homage to these individuals by preserving their residences as part of the nation's heritage. Several artworks illustrate and commemorate the birthplaces of second U.S. president John Adams and sixth U.S. President John Quincy Adams. A scene of the Ford Mansion at Morristown National Historical Park depicts Washington's winter headquarters during the Revolutionary War. The Mansion was also a treasured family home. The Grant-Kohrs Ranch scene captures the aura of cattle ranching and its role in the settlement of the American West. The serene water view of Campobello, Franklin and Eleanor Roosevelt's summer home, is a testament to the power of place and memory that this genre of painting provides.

Homes are powerful and sacred spaces. They often serve as a monument to the American heroes who inhabited them. In 1865, masses of mourners flocked to Abraham Lincoln's Springfield residence to honor him and his dream of a society free of slavery.

The views of home in this gallery provide the viewer with an immediate connection to its occupants, eminent Americans celebrated by the National Park Service and the nation.

(Johnny Grant's Home and Trading Post)
Unknown Artist
ca. 1866
Photograph of pencil on paper original.
W 24.6, H 17.9 cm
Grant-Kohrs Ranch National Historic Site, GRKO 7051

Architect's Rendering of Glenmont
Henry Hudson Holly
ca. 1880
Pencil on silk. L 22.9, W 17.8 cm
Thomas Edison National Historical Park, EDIS 102915

Plains Train Depot
Kenneth P. Craig
ca. 2007
Watercolor on paper. L 41, W 51 cm
Jimmy Carter National Historic Site, JICA 6927

(Maryland Landscape)
Helen West Stewart Ridgely
ca. 1875
Watercolor on paper. H 17.3, W 26.3 cm
Hampton National Historic Site, HAMP 4450

President Lincoln's Home, Springfield, Illinois
Harper's Weekly
November 26, 1864
Ink on paper. H 27, W 40.2 cm
Lincoln Home National Historic Site, LIHO 6617

PRESIDENT LINCOLN'S HOME, SPRINGFIELD, ILLINOIS.

Arlington Spring
Elizabeth Moore Reid
ca. 1850
Oil on wood. L 57.5, W 45 cm
Arlington House, The Robert E. Lee Memorial, ARHO 1883

Campobello
Albert Henry Munsell
1890
Oil on panel. H 50.8, W 66 cm
Home of Franklin D. Roosevelt
National Historic Site, HOFR 167

Portrait of the Old House in 1849
Godfrey N. Frankenstein
1849
Oil on canvas. L 61, W 92.7 cm
Adams National Historical Park, ADAM 8451

**Birthplaces of the Presidents John Adams and
John Quincy Adams**
Godfrey N. Frankenstein
1849
Oil on canvas. H 41.3, W 60.9 cm
Adams National Historical Park, ADAM 8453

WASHINGTON'S HEAD QUARTERS AT MORRISTOWN, N. J.

Washington's Head Quarters at Morristown, N.J.
Unknown Artist
1837
Ink on paper. L 10.9, W 18.2 cm
Morristown National Historical Park, MORR 8

Lewis Miller Birthplace
Jonathan Bradley Morse
ca. 1880
Oil on canvas. L 28, W 55.9 cm
Thomas Edison National Historical Park, EDIS 102579

Hyde Park
Johann Hermann Carmiencke
1856
Oil on canvas. L 44.5, W 65.4 cm
Vanderbilt Mansion National Historic Site, VAMA 5021

(Four Ridgely Cousins on the Hampton Estate with the Mansion's Cupola in the Background)
John Carlin
1856
Oil on canvas. H 49.8, W 60.9 cm
Hampton National Historic Site, HAMP 1128

Under Mannen Bridge in the Fukagawa Katsushika Hokusai, ca. 1830 | Woodblock on paper. L 24.3, W 36.3 cm | Carl Sandburg Home National Historic Site, CARL 47696

Personal Taste

"… the private home is the foundation of the public state … there is no better means of measuring … artistic culture than by examining … the arrangements of his house …"

Harriet Spofford, Art Decoration Applied to Furniture, 1878

The home was a symbol of wealth and power. It was the place where influential individuals were able to display their taste and collecting preferences. The home provided a palette to demonstrate achievement and refinement. Public spaces in the home, such as the drawing room, dining room, and library were often lavishly furnished and filled with well-crafted furniture, sculpture, mementos, and refined works of art. Aesthetic and decorating choices were seen as reflections of social class and the prevailing cultural taste of the period.

The paintings, sketches, and artworks on paper that distinguished Americans chose to decorate their homes reveal personal taste in an intimate and direct way. They provide a window into the private lives of public figures.

The artworks reveal wide-ranging pursuits and pleasures. They span the collecting of Japanese lithographs that decorated the home of Carl Sandburg in Flat Rock, North Carolina, to images of birds that Mrs. Thomas A. Edison displayed in her New Jersey home, to various scenes of favorite outdoor activities and travel abroad. Others reflect how the prevailing taste of the time can sometimes be acquired —— such as the way in which Edison acquired the bulk of his art collection when he purchased the fully furnished Glenmont estate. He said, "To think that it was possible to buy a place like this, which a man with taste for art and a talent for decoration had put ten years of enthusiastic study and effort into— the idea fairly turned my head and I snapped it up …"

The domestic sphere of spouses, children, and family pets, rather than politics and public life, prevailed in the home. Personal interests and collecting passions guided the selection of works of art exhibited in the various rooms. Paintings and drawings were done by friends and family members, some of whom were professional artists, and these were equally treasured, as seen in the Longfellow House and Arlington House, The Robert E. Lee Memorial collections. They provide an opportunity decades and centuries later to admire and enjoy the personal choices made by well-known public figures and their families in the original setting of their homes.

(Group of Men by a Smoky Fire)
Katsushika Hokusai
ca. 1830
Woodblock print on paper. L 25.4, W 36.9 cm
Carl Sandburg Home National Historic Site, CARL 47697

(Landscape of Swiss Chalet)
Clara Barton (attributed)
ca. 1869
Charcoal on paper. H 29.5, W 40.6 cm
Clara Barton National Historic Site, CLBA 540

River Landscape Ernest Wadsworth Longfellow, 1875 | Oil on canvas. H 46, W 57.9 cm
Longfellow House - Washington's Headquarters National Historic Site, LONG 4605

(White Flowers)
George Washington Carver
ca. 1930s
Oil on linen. H 133, W 68.5 cm
Tuskegee Institute National Historic Site, TUIN 1221

(Lakeside Village of St. Gilgen)
Myles Birket Foster
1853
Watercolor on paper. H 47.6, W 58.7 cm
Longfellow House - Washington's Headquarters
National Historic Site, LONG 4384

(Woodland Scene at Dusk)
Edmund Clarence Messer
1893–1894
Oil on canvas. L 145.4, W 120 cm
Frederick Douglass National Historic Site, FRDO 122

(Stream with Wooded Banks)
Unknown Artist
ca. 1890–1910
Oil on board. L 21.6, W 14.6 cm
Harry S Truman National Historic Site, HSTR 23679

Winter, St. Louis Creek
Dwight David Eisenhower
1955
Oil on canvas. L 60, W 49.4 cm
Eisenhower National Historic Site, EISE 9293

(Cornish Landscape) George de Forest Brush, 1872 | Oil on canvas. L 11.75, W 14 cm | Saint-Gaudens National Historic Site, SAGA 1

Lake Bank Birches
Wallace Nutting
ca. 1922
Hand colored Platinotype. L 31.1, W 37.5
Harry S Truman National Historic Site, HSTR 25168

Puerto Rican Jody
Frances W. Horne
Before 1925
Watercolor on paper. L 20.4, W 12.7 cm
Thomas Edison National Historical Park, EDIS 103462

(Wooded Walk and Meadows, possibly the Galleria Di Sopra at Albano) George Loring Brown, 1859 | Oil on canvas. H 48.9, W 66 cm
Longfellow House - Washington's Headquarters National Historic Site, LONG 4306

Pastoral Landscapes

"... I long for rural and domestic scenes, for the warbling of Birds ... As much as I converse with Sages and Heroes, they have very little of my Love or Admiration ..."

John Adams to Abigail Adams, 1777

Over the centuries, pastoral subject matter has been expressed through fine art, poetry, music, and literature. In ancient Rome, the poet Virgil stimulated interest in the pastoral genre as he described the idyllic life of the country shepherd. Many of his poems were set in a utopian land known as Arcadia. Romanticized and idealized landscapes that captured people and animals in harmony with nature were often described as "Arcadian."

Virgil's writings inspired several fourteenth century Italian poets, including Petrarch, who commented on the need to escape the clamor of towns and to find solace and quiet in the countryside. Interest in bucolic scenes expanded rapidly throughout Renaissance Europe.

There was a great fascination with pastoral images in the nineteenth century, most notably in France, England, and Germany. Influences included the great Dutch and Flemish masters, who considered the cow to be a symbol of prosperity.

American artists also contributed to the growing popularity of pastorals. Works depicting the idyllic countryside, noble peasants, cattle, and flocks of sheep provided an escape from rapidly urbanizing cities.

Artists explored the idealization of untouched nature and simple country landscapes in serene settings that were depicted without any of the damaging effects of industrial progress. Ironically, the artworks in this genre were often favored by wealthy patrons who had made their fortunes in noisy and crowded towns and cities but longed for life in the country.

Cattle and Landscape William Hart, ca. 1880 | Oil on canvas. L 61, W 50.8 cm
Thomas Edison National Historical Park, EDIS 102334

The Evening Hour
Thomas Bigelow Craig
ca. 1890
Watercolor on paper. L 77.6, W 62.3 cm
Cumberland Island National Seashore, CUIS 3404

(Village in the Countryside)
John Baptiste Camille Corot
1860–1870
Oil on board. H 53.3, W 64.8 cm
Longfellow House - Washington's
Headquarters National Historic Site, LONG 4332

Landscape with Peasants Michele Pagano (attributed), ca. 1725 | Oil on canvas. H 149.9, W 204.47 | Hampton National Historic Site, HAMP 873

(View of Morristown ca. 1850–1860 from the Hill behind the First Presbyterian Church)
Edward Kranich
1855
Oil on canvas. H 91.4, L 66 cm
Morristown National Historical Park, MORR 3257

View of the Alps
Augusta Fisher Homer Saint-Gaudens
ca. 1880s
Oil on canvas. L 38, W 30 cm
Saint-Gaudens National Historic Site, SAGA 4766

Light In the Forest
Julian Alden Weir
ca. 1907–1910
Oil on wood. L 63.3, W 49.3 cm
Weir Farm National Historic Site, WEFA 2935

Landscape
Frank Chickering Warren
n.d.
Oil on canvas. H 56.5, W 70.5 cm
Vanderbilt Mansion National Historic Site, VAMA 314

Romantic Landscape
Edmund Darch Lewis
1854
Oil on canvas. L 180.3, W 130.8 cm
Vanderbilt Mansion National Historic Site, VAMA 192

Spring Landscape, Branchville Julian Alden Weir, 1882 | Watercolor on paper. L 12.7, W 17.1 cm | Weir Farm National Historic Site, WEFA 2934

Clam Gatherers Edward Moran, 1875–1880 | Oil on canvas. L 66, W 107 cm | Marsh - Billings - Rockefeller National Historical Park, MABI 1568

Waterscapes

"All that is within me cries out to go back to my home on the Hudson River."

Franklin Delano Roosevelt

Throughout history, people have gravitated to waterways. Creeks, lagoons, lakes, rivers, and the sea provide sustenance, convenience, strategic location, and great beauty. Depictions of these vistas can be fierce and foreboding or calm and serene. Scenes of rocky coastlines and sandy beaches or vessels at sea have long been a popular subject for artists. The many ways humans relate to bodies of water for recreation, industry, development, and warfare have provided artists with inspiration and a wide range of subjects to commit to canvas.

Although landscape paintings were extremely popular in the late nineteenth and early twentieth centuries, waterscapes or marine paintings also had great fascination for art collectors. At this time, wealthy families regularly traveled domestically. They often journeyed to cooler climates during the hot and humid summers, with mountain resorts and the seaside as frequent destinations. Many built summer homes where they would spend several months every year. These homes were filled with decorative and fine arts, including ones of marine subjects.

Nostalgia for youthful and languid summers at the beach, lakeside idylls, and transatlantic journeys fueled the collecting of maritime paintings. Works that depicted aquatic scenes were considered the appropriate decorating choices for less formal and more relaxed viewing.

Depictions of raging and brooding seas pitted humans against the might and fury of nature. Artworks that captured the fluidity of coastal waters and sunsets at the water's edge conveyed a sense of calm and serenity that made them eminently collectible. Seascapes graced the Edison home at Glenmont, New Jersey and were highly favored by the Carnegie family at their summer home on Cumberland Island. Tranquil seascapes were also enjoyed by the Billings and Rockefellers in their Vermont home.

Maritime works of art in the San Francisco Maritime National Historical Park collections reflect America's golden age of sailing, when the nation's success in war and trade greatly depended upon its sailing vessels. These paintings document the commercial story of an earlier age when sailing ships moved tons of cargo that fueled the nation's economy. Another genre of marine painting includes the recording of significant naval battles that also provide handsome and accurate renderings of technical details of the ships themselves. Maritime art continues to reflect the endless fascination with the sea and its related activities.

Refuge from the Storm
Theodore Alexander Weber
ca. 1880
Watercolor on paper. L 59.1, W 44.3 cm
Cumberland Island National Seashore, CUIS 1704

Woman at Water's Edge
Peter Possart
ca. 1902
Oil on canvas. L 110.6, W 86.5 cm
Cumberland Island National Seashore, CUIS 3403

Storm at Sea or Mid-Ocean, Moonlight
Thomas Moran
1920
Oil on canvas. H 77.3, W 102.3 cm
National Park Service,
Museum Management Program, WASO 1448

Rocky Coast Scene
Samuel Peter Rolt Triscott
Before 1925
Watercolor on paper. L 68.6, W 40.7 cm
Thomas Edison National Historical Park, EDIS 102826

Fishing Boats off Coast
Charles Henry Ebert
1924–1930
Oil on canvas. L 50.8, W 63.5 cm
Thomas Edison National Historical Park, EDIS 102373

(Lone Figure Walking at the Water's Edge)
John Joseph Enneking
1877
Oil on canvas. H 35.9, W 53.7 cm
Longfellow House - Washington's Headquarters
National Historic Site, LONG 6769

(Rowboat with Four Seamen and their Catch)
Eugène Louis Gabriel Isabey
1825–1835
Oil on canvas. H 65.4, W 81.7 cm
Longfellow House - Washington's Headquarters
National Historic Site, LONG 4333

From Eikvåg
Nicolai Martin Ulfsten
1875–1885
Oil on canvas. H 58.4, W 82 cm
Longfellow House - Washington's Headquarters
National Historic Site, LONG 4711

Fishing Boats at Sunset Théodore Gudin, 1850–1870 | Oil on canvas. H 52.7, W 61.9 cm
Longfellow House - Washington's Headquarters National Historic Site, LONG 4126

(San Francisco Waterfront)
Chris Jorgensen
ca. 1898
Oil on canvas. H 59, W 90 cm
San Francisco Maritime
National Historical Park, SAFR 21348

(San Francisco Harbor in 1849)
Unknown Artist
ca. 1849
Oil on canvas. H 61.6, W 73.7 cm
San Francisco Maritime
National Historical Park, SAFR 5058

(Grounding of the Steamer Alameda on the Rocks at Fort Point, San Francisco)
Thomas Colb
1905
Oil on canvas. H 22.2, W 36 cm
San Francisco Maritime
National Historical Park, SAFR 12770

(Golden Gate Looking out to Sea Before Construction of the Golden Gate Bridge)
Unknown Artist
1914
Watercolor on paper. H 26, W 54.5 cm
San Francisco Maritime
National Historical Park, SAFR 3866

**The Olive Branch Tendered to the World but
Enforced by the Sword of Justice and Might Beneath**
Pinckney Marcius-Simons
1904
Oil on canvas. L 45.7, W 35.6 cm
Sagamore Hill National Historic Site, SAHI 528

Porcelain Towers
Pinckney Marcius-Simons
ca. 1900
Oil on canvas. L 88.9, W 113 cm
Sagamore Hill National Historic Site, SAHI 541

Cliff House and Bay of San Francisco Albert Bierstadt, 1871–1872 | Oil on canvas. L 44, W 75 cm
Marsh - Billings - Rockefeller National Historical Park, MABI 4422

On the Trail in Idaho Peter Moran 1879–1880 | Oil on panel. L 15, W 35.5 cm | Marsh - Billings - Rockefeller National Historical Park, MABI 2868

American Experiences

American Experiences

"Those who contemplate the beauty of the earth find resources of strength that will endure as long as life lasts." Rachel Carson

The landscape features in many works of art that document the human condition and human experiences. Most of the artworks in this gallery are not traditional landscape paintings. However, all include some element or representation of nature, the countryside, the great outdoors, habitat, or water bound by land. Nature is present in each, from formal portraits of General George Washington framed by trees or leading soldiers into battle, to solitary figures dwarfed by the Southwestern landscape.

Artists have captured intense experiences, often romanticized, from quiet contemplation of a sunset on horseback, to the excitement of westward travel. Mountains, trees, and expanses of plains and skies frame the people within them. In some artworks, the landscape is brimming with tension. In others, a serene calm is conveyed. Fields and forests form a backdrop to idealized scenes of soldiers preparing for their next military engagement.

The soothing greenery of the countryside and everyday activities in and around camp convey comfort and familiarity that belie the horror that awaits in the next battle. Other works poignantly depict the freedom of distant vistas that are visible beyond the painful confines of the internment camp.

People are depicted within and at one with nature and the landscape. Artists have skillfully frozen action and movement of individuals and wildlife in the expanses of the great outdoors. Travelers are almost overpowered by looming mountains, endless plains, and canyon walls. The artist has keenly observed and recorded the direct gaze of individuals enveloped in nature. Others move silently on the land in the haze of dusk and provide the viewer with a regenerative calm.

Artists in the Gallery and in Park Collections

Alcatraz Island, Golden Gate National Recreation Area artwork in this gallery includes works by inmate John Paul Chase when Alcatraz was a Federal penitentiary.

Andersonville National Historic Site collections relate to the Andersonville prison, other prisoner-of-war camps, and to the Civil War and later conflicts. The lithograph in this gallery is by Lieutenant T. A. Prime. *Artists represented in the collection* include Vaughn Adams, Carl V. Cossins, Curtis G. Davis, Donald J. Larson, Thomas Odea, Rodney J. Rousselle, Angelo M. Spinelli, and others.

Bandelier National Monument artwork in this gallery is by Pablita Velarde of Santa Clara Pueblo, who produced over 70 paintings to help visitors understand the ancestral Pueblo sites in the park.

Cape Cod National Seashore collections relate to the seashore and cultural landscapes and Cape Cod's past and continuing ways of life. *Artists represented in the collection* are Abbot Graves, Elizabeth Hayes Pratt, and Stow Wegenroth.

Gettysburg National Military Park collections relate to the Battle of Gettysburg and the Civil War. Artwork in this gallery is by William R. McIlvaine, Jr. *Artists represented in the collection* include John Chester Buttre, Theodore R. Davis, Edwin Forbes, George L. Frankenstein, John Worthington Mansfield, Edwin J. Meeker, Alexander H. Ritchie, William Ludwell Sheppard, Isaac Walton Taber, William H. Tipton, Don Troiani, James Walker, and others.

Grand Canyon National Park artwork in this gallery is by Louis Benton Akin. See the *America's Treasured Places* gallery for artists represented in the collection.

Hampton National Historic Site see the *Eminent Americans at Home* gallery for artists represented in the collection.

Home of Franklin D. Roosevelt National Historic Site artwork in this gallery is by Thomas Birch and Casimir Clayton Griswold. See the *Eminent Americans at Home* gallery for artists represented in the collection.

Hubbell Trading Post National Historic Site collections relate to Juan Lorenzo Hubbell, who welcomed many artists to his home and trading post in Ganado, Arizona. Artists in this gallery are Carl Oscar Borg, Maynard Lafayette Dixon, Albert Lorey Groll, C. Bertram Hartman, John Warner Norton, and Tschudy aka Herbert Bolivar Judy. *Artists represented in the collection* include M. W. Batchellar, Harold Harrington Betts, Elbridge Ayer Burbank, William Robinson Leigh, Edgar Alwyn Payne, William (Wilhelm) Frederick Ritschel, Warren Eliphalet Rollins, and others.

Independence National Historical Park collections include portraits of leading figures of the American Revolution and eighteenth century American period furnishings, objects, and documents relating to Independence Hall. Artwork in this gallery is by James Peale. *Artists represented in the collection* include Ralph Earl, Jacob Eichholtz, David Rent Etter, Robert Feke, Henry Inman, James Read Lambdin, Edward Dalton Marchant, Samuel F. B. Morse, Bass Otis, Charles Willson Peale, Rembrandt Peale, Robert Edge Pine, Charles Peale Polk, Ellen Sharples, Felix Sharples, James Sharples, Jr., James Sharples, Sr., Gilbert Stuart, Ellen Oldmixon Sully, Thomas Sully, Benjamin Trott, Benjamin West, John Woodside, and others.

Jefferson National Expansion Memorial artwork in this gallery is by Carl Bodmer. See the *America's Treasured Places* gallery for artists in the collection.

Manzanar National Historic Site and its collections tell the painful story of relocation and confinement of Japanese Americans from 1942–1945. Artwork in this gallery is by Henry Masasuke Kumano, Hideo Kobashigawa, and George Okazaki. *Artists represented in the collection* include F. Okamoto, Kango Takamura, and others.

Marsh - Billings - Rockefeller National Historical Park artwork in this gallery is by Albert Bierstadt, William Parsons Winchester Dana, Charles Théodore Frère, Peter Moran, and Frank Waller. See *The American Conservation Movement and the Hudson River School* gallery for artists in the collection.

Morristown National Historical Park collections relate to the American Revolutionary War, with eighteenth century Philadelphia and New York furniture and Washingtonia, including Washington's Masonic sash and Inaugural Ball suit, documents, and Mount Vernon farm journals. Artwork in this gallery includes work by John Chester Buttre, Imogene Robinson, and Robert Shaw. See the *Eminent Americans at Home* gallery for artists represented in the collection.

Natchez National Historical Park collections are associated with planter families including the McMurran family and the two-story Greek-Revival structure on the Melrose Estate, ca. 1845–1865 in Natchez, Mississippi. Artists in this gallery are William H. Baker and James Hamilton Shegogue . *Artists represented in the collection* include Phyllis Dennison, James Hamilton, Guiseppe Magni, Martin Pate, Alphonse Sesport, Giuseppe Signorini, and others.

National Park Service, Museum Management Program artwork in this gallery is by Eugene Kingman, Thomas Moran, and Walter Alois Weber.

Nez Perce National Historical Park includes Nez Perce and Plains Indians materials such as baskets, woven bags, feathered items, and beadwork. Artwork in this gallery is by Kevin Peters. *Artists represented in the collection* include Rowena Alcorn, Eve Rockwell Little, Nakia Williamson, and others.

Sagamore Hill National Historic Site artwork in this gallery is by Arthur Burdett Frost and an unknown artist in the Vatican workshop. See the *America's Treasured Places* gallery for other artists in the collection.

Saint-Gaudens National Historic Site artwork in this gallery is by Augusta Fisher Homer Saint-Gaudens. See the *Eminent Americans at Home* gallery for other artists in the collection.

Scotts Bluff National Monument collections relate to the history of the Oregon Trail and include photographs, sketches and watercolors by William Henry Jackson, a member of the Hayden Geological Survey of 1871. As a soldier during the Civil War, Jackson documented daily life in and nearby camp.

Thomas Edison National Historical Park gallery includes work by T. McKay. See the *Eminent Americans at Home* gallery for other artists in the collection.

Yosemite National Park artwork in this gallery includes work by Benjamin Willard Sears. See the *America's Treasured Places* gallery for other artists in the collection.

(Pueblo Colorado Wash north of the Hubbell Trading Post with Hubbell Hill visible on the left) Carl Oscar Borg, 1916
Watercolor on paper. H 12.7, W 17.2 cm | Hubbell Trading Post National Historic Site, HUTR 2316

And The Sun Went Down (Arizona Desert) Albert Lorey Groll, n.d. | Oil on canvas. L 21.6, W 26.6 cm
Hubbell Trading Post National Historic Site, HUTR 3427

Experiencing Nature

"In every walk with nature one receives far more than he seeks" John Muir

Artworks in this gallery depict the human figure in relation to, and intertwined with, nature and the landscape. Americans' interest in experiencing nature was widely expressed in nineteenth century art and literature. Nature inspired the Hudson River School artists to explore their country and paint realistic and spiritual scenes of the American landscape.

Nature also inspired many of that century's great writers, including Henry David Thoreau, Emily Dickinson, Ralph Waldo Emerson, and Walt Whitman. These writers, influenced by Transcendentalism, experienced a natural world that was highly spiritual. The divine could be experienced through nature.

The portraits of Martha Washington and of the Nez Perce woman face forward, gazing directly at the viewer from within the landscape. Both are enveloped in nature. The two children from Natchez are in repose and are surrounded by dark undergrowth and trees. In these works, nature and vegetation are a significant and dominating presence that frame the individuals depicted.

Southwestern landscapes place people into stark terrain of vast mesas and towering canyons. As people and animals move through the landscape, all seem to be at one with their surroundings. The warm light and saturated colors capture the deep interconnection between the artist, their subjects, and the land. From the vigorous activity of rabbit hunting to the slow journey of the horse-led wagon in the narrow canyon, nature serves to provide a consoling pleasure.

The quiet serenity of the landscape and direct experience of nature is therapeutic. This genre of art allowed viewers the regenerative calm of the countryside from within their own homes, especially for city dwellers in the midst of restless and ever-expanding cities.

Beginning in the twentieth century, environmental literature, inspired by great landscape art, increasingly emphasized the need to take an active role in preserving nature to be good citizens and stewards. These efforts have inspired generations of Americans who enjoy the beauty and experience of nature and who work to preserve it. The works of art capture the range of emotion from a sense of solitude to exciting adventure.

The Steamer Yellowstone on the 9th April 1833 Carl Bodmer, 1840 | Aquatint engraving. L 63, W 46 cm
Jefferson National Expansion Memorial, JEFF 4767

Snags (sunken trees) on the Missouri Carl Bodmer, ca. 1839–1840 | Aquatint engraving. L 60, W 42.9 cm
Jefferson National Expansion Memorial, JEFF 4769

A Bit of Old Santa Fe Trail Albert Lorey Groll, ca. 1900 | Watercolor on board. H 37.5, W 42.5 cm
Hubbell Trading Post National Historic Site, HUTR 2309

Facing Page

Rabbit Hunt
Pablita Velarde
ca. 1940
Casein paint on masonite. L 37.8, W 20.5 cm
Bandelier National Monument, BAND 654

Men and Boys Herding Town Horses
Pablita Velarde
ca. 1940
Casein paint on masonite. L 38, W 20 cm
Bandelier National Monument, BAND 655

Desert Showers Maynard Lafayette Dixon, 1907
Oil on canvas. L 50.8, W 76.2 cm. Hubbell Trading Post National Historic Site, HUTR 3510

Canyon del Muerto, #2 John Warner Norton, n.d. | Oil on canvas. H 56, W 35.5 cm
Hubbell Trading Post National Historic Site, HUTR 7497

Talking Rock, Canyon de Chelly C. Bertram Hartman, 1916 | Oil on canvas. L 43, W 30.2 cm
Hubbell Trading Post National Historic Site, HUTR 3508

Hubbell Hill Tschudy aka Herbert Bolivar Judy, n.d. | Oil on canvas. L 40.7, W 53.5 cm | Hubbell Trading Post National Historic Site, HUTR 3511

El Tovar Louis Benton Akin, After 1906 | Chromolithograph on paper. W 86, H 39 cm | Grand Canyon National Park, GRCA 22770

(Indian Camp at Night) Benjamin Willard Sears, ca. 1880s | Oil on canvas. L 53, W 64.2 cm | Yosemite National Park, YOSE 68133

Frances Davis
William H. Baker (attributed)
ca. 1850
Oil on canvas. H 100.3, W 74.9 cm
Natchez National Historical Park, NATC 115

Stephen Kelly
James Hamilton Shegogue
ca. 1855
Oil on canvas. H 109.2, W 149.9 cm
Natchez National Historical Park, NATC 25

Martha Washington
Mezzotint by John Folwell and drawn by W. Oliver Stone
after the original by John Woolaston
Engraved, printed, and published by J.C. Buttre, New York
1863
Ink on paper. L 86.4, W 66 cm
Morristown National Historical Park, MORR 121

**Sometimes, During a Summer Storm,
Her Hair Ran with Rainbows**
Kevin Peters
1992
Acrylic on canvas. L 76, W 61 cm
Nez Perce National Historical Park, NEPE 34566

The Provision Train Painted by Imogene Robinson, Engraved by C. Tomkins, ca. 1877 | Ink on paper. L 76.8, W 48.3 cm
Morristown National Historical Park, MORR 182

Conflict

"Soldiering was 99% boredom and 1% sheer terror" Civil War Soldier's Letter

Art depicting conflict has a long tradition, from murals and stelae of the ancient world to contemporary armies engaged in mechanized and deadly encounters. Works of art in this genre cover a wide range of military topics. They present heroic scenes of soldiers in combat, defeated enemies, bound and humiliated hostages, and the aftermath of battle. Naval engagements were a popular genre. Accurate renditions of uniforms reflected a keen interest in the military and were also popular.

The artworks in this gallery are not all heroic visions of warfare. Several present the more human aspects of conflict. They depict officers, enlisted men and townspeople within the landscape, engaged in daily and sometimes mundane activities.

There are several renditions of the Revolutionary War hero, General Washington. In one, he is portrayed on horseback leading his troops into battle. Another, by James Peale, presents the general with detailed attention to his uniform. The artist included two uniformed and armed men, James and Charles Willson Peale, who stand behind Washington's right shoulder under a tree, possibly as a reference to the brothers' Revolutionary War experience. A column of uniformed soldiers, one carrying the French flag, is seen in the right mid-ground.

For the average soldier during the Civil War, army life was hard. Torn from the comforts of their homes, men and boys of military age were suddenly subjected to rigid discipline, strict routine, poor diet, sickness, and inadequate shelter. During these long periods in camp, soldiers found ways to express themselves through art and other pursuits. Sketching with pencil or pen allowed absent husbands, brothers, and sons to enclose scenes of camp life in letters home to family and friends.

There are rare first person renderings of soldiers in camp by trained artists. The young William Henry Jackson was a skilled observer and artist when he enlisted in Company K of the 12th Vermont Infantry of the Union Army in 1862. He recorded his fellow soldiers in camp, as well as places nearby. Private William McIlvaine, Jr., of the 5th New York Infantry Regiment was a professional artist before he enlisted. It is fortunate that his commanding officer gave him permission " … to paint … and … get excused from any duties …" so that daily life in camp can be viewed more than a century and half after the Civil War.

Naval Engagement, War of 1812
Thomas Birch (attributed)
1813
Oil on canvas. H 58, W 73 cm
Home of Franklin D. Roosevelt National Historic Site, HOFR 227

U.S.S. "Constitution" Leaving New York Harbor
Thomas Birch
ca. 1813
Oil on canvas. H 76, W 88 cm
Home of Franklin D. Roosevelt National Historic Site, HOFR 850

Naval Engagement, War of 1812
Thomas Birch (attributed)
1813
Oil on canvas H 70.1, W 60.1 cm
Home of Franklin D. Roosevelt National Historic Site, HOFR 226

Ship in Breeze of a Rocky Coast
Thomas Birch
1844
Oil on canvas. H 77.5, W 97.8 cm
Home of Franklin D. Roosevelt National Historic Site, HOFR 2076

George Washington James Peale, 1787–1790 | Oil on canvas. H 92.7, W 70.8 cm
Independence National Historical Park, INDE 14171

Washington Headquarters, Morristown, NJ Robert Shaw (signed remarque proof), 1910 | Ink on paper. H 23.8, W 34.3 cm
Morristown National Historic Park, MORR 45

Camp Cooking, Wolf Run Shoal
William Henry Jackson
1863
Pencil on paper. H 18, W 22 cm
Scotts Bluff National Monument, SCBL 253

Winter Quarters, Wolf Run Shoals, Va. 1863
William Henry Jackson
1863
Pencil on paper. H 18, W 23.5 cm
Scotts Bluff National Monument, SCBL 233

McLane's Ford, Bull Run, Va.
William Henry Jackson
June 10, 1863
Pencil on paper. H 18, W 25 cm
Scotts Bluff National Monument, SCBL 267

Picket Guard Near Falmouth, VA, March 17, 1863 William McIlvaine Jr., 1863 | Watercolor on paper. H 15.9, W 24.2 cm
Gettysburg National Military Park, GETT 31203

Camp Opposite House of Dr. Crut
William McIlvaine Jr.
1862
Watercolor on paper. H 16.5, W 26 cm
Gettysburg National Military Park, GETT 31202

Negro Quarters, White House, May 17, 1862
William McIlvaine Jr.
1862
Watercolor on paper. H 14.3, W 24.2 cm
Gettysburg National Military Park, GETT 31193

At Camp Lockmoor - Near Newton Nov 17, 1861
William McIlvaine Jr.
1861
Watercolor on paper. H 16.5, W 23.3 cm
Gettysburg National Military Park, GETT 31192

Camp on James River, VA, July 6, 1862, Tent of Col. Buchanan
William McIlvaine Jr.
1862
Watercolor on paper. H 16.8, W 25.4 cm
Gettysburg National Military Park, GETT 31204

Manzanar Barracks with Snow Covered Sierra Nevada Mountains Henry Masasuke Kumano, 1944 | Oil on board. L 70, W 54.5 cm
Manzanar National Historic Site, MANZ 5171

Confinement

"We had about one week to dispose of what we owned, except what we could pack and carry for our departure by bus … for Manzanar …" William Hohri, Manzanar Internee

The National Park Service preserves several sites associated with confinement. Japan's attack on Pearl Harbor on December 7, 1941 led the United States into World War II and radically changed the lives of men, women, and children of Japanese ancestry living in the United States. More than 100,000 Japanese Americans were forcibly removed from their homes and businesses and confined without due process from 1942 to 1945.

Manzanar National Historical Site, located near the base of the Sierra Nevada in California, housed 10,000 individuals. Arts and craft clubs provided opportunities to share knowledge and culture during confinement. Artists gave lessons in painting and sketching, and provided their own equipment and supplies. The classes allowed internees to pass the time while creating beauty in the bleak camps.

Many of the instructors had been successful artists before being interned at Manzanar. Their work documented life in the camp and captured the looming power of the Sierra Nevada Mountains rising dramatically to the west of camp.

Alcatraz Island, the most famous Federal prison in U.S. history, housed some of America's most notorious Federal offenders from 1934 to 1963. They were held under the most secure and regimented conditions, in the virtually escape-proof environment on a rocky island in the middle of San Francisco Bay. When not occupied in work programs, inmates spent time in recreational activities—including art projects. Inmates behind impenetrable prison walls created exuberant and brightly colored paintings of San Francisco's skyline.

Andersonville prison camp in Georgia was one of the largest Confederate military prisons during the Civil War. More than 45,000 Union soldiers were confined at Andersonville and close to 13,000 died there. Artwork produced under the harsh conditions of war provided an opportunity to keep inmates occupied in the most tragic of situations.

(Panoramic View from Alcatraz of Telegraph Hill with Coit Tower), Panel 1
John Paul Chase
1950–1955
Oil on board. W 50.9, H 40.6 cm
Alcatraz Island, Golden Gate National Recreation Area,
GOGA 18466

(Panoramic View from Alcatraz of Aquatic Park and Black Point Areas), Panel 3
John Paul Chase
1950–1955
Oil on board. W 50.8, H 40.7 cm
Alcatraz Island, Golden Gate National Recreation Area,
GOGA 18468

(Panoramic View from Alcatraz of San Francisco Waterfront, from Taylor to Larkin Streets, and the Cannery and the Hyde Street Pier), Panel 2
John Paul Chase
1950–1955
Oil on board. W 50.8, H 40.7 cm
Alcatraz Island, Golden Gate National Recreation Area,
GOGA 18467

(Panoramic View from Alcatraz of Piers at Fort Mason, the Port of Embarcation), Panel 4
John Paul Chase
1950–1955
Oil on board. W 50.8, H 40.7 cm
Alcatraz Island, Golden Gate National Recreation Area,
GOGA 18469

Mt. Williamson and the Manzanar Barracks Henry Masasuke Kumano, 1945 | Oil on board. W 99, H 35 cm
Manzanar National Historic Site, MANZ 7578

Manzanar Barracks
George Okazaki
ca. 1942–1946
Watercolor on paper. H 21.5, W 30.2 cm
Manzanar National Historic Site, MANZ 2224

Manzanar Woodblock
Hideo Kobashigawa
1944
Pigment on rice paper. L 30.5, W 45.7 cm
Manzanar National Historic Site, MANZ 7545

THE PRISON PEN AT MILLEN, GA., AS IT APPEARED PREVIOUS TO THE ARRIVAL OF GENERAL SHERMAN'S ARMY.—FROM A SKETCH BY LIEUTENANT T. A. PRIME.

The Prison Pen at Millen Ga., as it Appeared Previous to the Arrival of General Sherman's Army, From a Sketch by Lieutenant T. A. Prime
Lieutenant T. A. Prime, ca. 1880 | Ink on paper. L 50.8, W 40.7 cm | Andersonville National Historic Site, ANDE 3151

Egyptian Life Frank Waller, ca. 1878 | Oil on panel. L 24, W 34 cm | Marsh - Billings - Rockefeller National Historical Park, MABI 2873

Americans Abroad

"Though we travel the world over to find the beautiful, we must carry it with us or we find it not."

Ralph Waldo Emerson

Many affluent Americans appreciated nature and landscapes beyond the borders of America. They had the wealth to travel abroad for business as well as for pleasure. As was typical of their English counterparts, wealthy Americans took extended "Grand Tours" of Europe. These included visits to Austria, Belgium, France, Germany, Greece, Italy, and Switzerland.

Long stays in Rome and Paris were often arranged. Most collected souvenirs to remind them of the places they had visited. As a young woman, Julia Parmly Billings did the Grand Tour with her mother and visited art museums in Dresden, Florence, Venice, and London. In her 1855 travel journal, Julia wrote, "… we saw such scores of fine pictures, that I must content myself with marking in the catalogue those that most impressed us … Leaving at 2 1/2 we came home, rested, then went to the porcelain store … where we bought large and small busts."

Americans spent time traveling absorbing European artworks and often enjoyed collecting art of earlier eras. These works were shipped home to America and prominently displayed in drawing and dining rooms of grand homes, making a statement about the taste and refinement of the owner.

Many collectors sought out "Orientalist" paintings that captured the mystery and attraction of far off lands, in particular, the Middle East and North Africa. These artworks depict exotic peoples, animals and the natural world.

The works featured in this gallery are likely souvenirs of travel, visual reminders of past journeys to Europe and the Middle East, and display a great interest in the beauty of the landscapes.

Canal in Cairo Charles Theodore Frère, 1870s | Oil, canvas. L 17, W 29 cm | Marsh - Billings - Rockefeller National Historical Park, MABI 2867

On the Nile
Charles Théodore Frère
ca. 1878
Oil on canvas. L 38.5, W 76 cm
Marsh - Billings - Rockefeller National Historical Park,
MABI 3931

Brittany Beach
William Parsons Winchester Dana
ca. 1865–1870
Oil on canvas. L 39, W 75.5 cm
Marsh - Billings - Rockefeller National Historical Park,
MABI 3932

**Vista Della Gran Festa Del Re Ferdinando IV Nel
Regnio Di Napoli A 17 Guignio [sic] 1815**
Unknown Artist
ca. 1820
Gouache on paper. H 56.8, W 83.8 cm
Hampton National Historic Site, HAMP 1084

Morning on Lake Trasimeno
Casimir Clayton Griswold
1880
Oil on canvas. H 61 , W 88.9 cm
Home of Franklin D. Roosevelt
National Historic Site, HOFR 150

The Matterhorn Albert Bierstadt, n.d. | Oil on canvas. L 100.5, W 70 cm
Marsh - Billings - Rockefeller National Historical Park, MABI 2844

Santa Margherita Della Salute, Grand Canal, Venice
T. McKay
Before 1925
Pastel on board. L 22.9, W 35.6 cm
Thomas Edison National Historic Site, EDIS 102632

Gardens of the Vatican
Unknown Artist in the Vatican workshop
Late 1890s
Mosaic. H 57.1, W 77.5 cm
Sagamore Hill National Historic Site, SAHI 574

Village and Castle of La Roche, Belgium
Augusta Fisher Homer Saint-Gaudens
ca. 1880s
Oil on canvas. L 37.5, W 26.2 cm
Saint-Gaudens National Historic Site, SAGA 4762

European Landscape Thomas Moran, 1920 | Oil on canvas. H 52.8, W 42.3 cm
National Park Service, Museum Management Program, WASO 1446

Rocky Mountain Big Horn Sheep Walter Alois Weber, Late 1930s | Oil on canvas. W 100, L 79.8 cm | National Park Service, Museum Management Program, WASOA 11

Wildlife in the Landscape

"Nature holds the beautiful, for the artist who has the insight to extract it"

Albrecht Durer (1471–1528)

The art of capturing animals in nature has a long tradition. The genre encompasses prehistoric animals moving across cave walls, ancient Roman mosaics of wild beasts of prey, animals of unusual proportions imagined by Renaissance artists, as well as John James Audubon's illustrations of birds and contemporary painters of wildlife in nature.

From the sixteenth century on, scientists and travelers sought to depict exotic wild animals while exploring the animal kingdom in relation to humans. John James Audubon (1785–1851), who had worked as a naturalist and taxidermist, observed and sketched animals in the field. His magnificent and accurate portraits of American birds, *Birds of America*, published between 1827 to 1838, were well received at the time and continue to be greatly prized.

Twentieth century wildlife artists were informed by close observation of animals, scientific data, as well as notes and sketches that were made in the field and in zoos and natural history museums. The works of art recorded appropriate animal behaviors and poses, as well as typical habitat and flora that conveyed a sense of realism that engaged and informed the viewer.

Many works in this gallery were painted by Walter Alois Weber. The accomplished wildlife artist was a trained zoologist, botanist and field collector. He was equally adept at painting grizzly bears in the wilds or birds in the trees of his backyard. Weber studied living animal subjects in the wild wherever possible, irrespective of species, so that he recorded the right color, movement and habitat.

Wildlife art captures the vigor of animals in the wild and brings a sense of intimacy and immediacy to the viewer. Today, national parks provide artists with the opportunity to observe animals in a natural setting and capture their beauty on canvas.

Beaver Hut on the Missouri Carl Bodmer, 1839 | Aquatint engraving. L 59.9, W 42.3 cm | Jefferson National Expansion Memorial, JEFF 4768

Grizzly Bears Walter Alois Weber, Late 1930s | Oil on canvas. L 80.3, W 59.4 cm | National Park Service, Museum Management Program, WASOA 40

California Condor Walter Alois Weber, Late 1930s | Oil on canvas. L 89.5, W 68.9 cm
National Park Service, Museum Management Program, WASOA 69

Cougar Walter Alois Weber, Late 1930s | Oil on canvas. W 100.5, L 69.5 cm | National Park Service, Museum Management Program, WASOA 66

Prairie Chickens
Walter Alois Weber
Late 1930s
Oil on canvas. L 81.3, W 51.5 cm
National Park Service,
Museum Management Program, WASOA 35

(Wolves Moving by Night)
Walter Alois Weber
ca. 1930s
Oil on canvas. L 100.5, W 80.7 cm
National Park Service,
Museum Management Program, WASOA 12

Ivory-Billed Woodpeckers
Walter Alois Weber
Late 1930s
Oil on canvas. L 45.7, W 61.2 cm
National Park Service,
Museum Management Program, WASOA 25

Mountain Goat
Walter Alois Weber
Late 1930s
Oil on canvas. L 78.5, W 137.5 cm
National Park Service,
Museum Management Program, WASOA 18

(Man with Horse and Dog with a Woman Boarding a Boat in the Background) Unknown Artist, ca. 1870–1880s
Oil on canvas. W 50, H 35 cm | Cape Cod National Seashore, CACO 3798

(Sage Fowl Shooting)
Arthur Burdett Frost
ca. 1885
Lithograph on paper. L 56.5, W 36.9 cm
Sagamore Hill National Historic Site, SAHI 1290

Shot at Mountain Ram
Arthur Burdett Frost
ca. 1885
Lithograph on paper. L 61, W 41.3 cm
Sagamore Hill National Historic Site, SAHI 1309

Grand Teton Eugene Kingman, ca. 1930s | Oil on canvas. L 91.5, W 112.3 cm
National Park Service, Museum Management Program, WASOA 46

Participating Parks Index

Artist Index

Sources

Essays in this book incorporate information from the National Park Service publications listed below.

Hitchcock, Ann. *NPS Museums 1904–2004*. <http://www.nps.gov/museum/centennial/> April 2004.

Lewis, Ralph. *Museum Curatorship in the National Park Service, 1904–1982*. Washington, DC: National Park Service, 1993.

McGrath, Robert L. *Art and the American Conservation Movement*. Special History Study, Northeast Museum Services Center. Boston: National Park Service, 2001.

National Park Service. *The National Parks: Shaping the System*. Produced by Harpers Ferry Center, 2005.

_____. *Museum Handbook, Part I, Museum Collections* Chapter 1: NPS Museums and Collections. Washington, DC: National Park Service. 2006.

_____. *Park Profiles* that summarize park museum collections at <www.nps.gov/museum>

_____. *Park Homepages* available through <www.nps.gov>

_____. *Virtual Exhibits* that feature park museum collections and virtual tours at <www.nps.gov/museum>

Credits

Laura Anderson, Curator, Marsh - Billings - Rockefeller National Historic Site

Beth Miller, Curator, Thomas Edison National Historical Park

National Park Service staff responsible for museum collections at over 45 National Parks